Whose Idea Was That?

Inventions that Changed Our Lives

Whose Idea Was That?
Inventions that Changed Our Lives
David Ellyard

First published in Australia in 2008 by
Young Reed
an imprint of New Holland Publishers (Australia) Pty Ltd
Sydney • Auckland • London • Cape Town

1/66 Gibbes St Chatswood NSW 2067 Australia
218 Lake Road Northcote Auckland 0627 New Zealand
86 Edgware Road London W2 2EA United Kingdom
80 McKenzie Street Cape Town 8001 South Africa

10 9 8 7 6 5 4 3 2 1

National Library of Australia Cataloguing-in-Publication Data:

Author: Ellyard, David, 1942-
Title: Whose idea was that? / David Ellyard.
Publisher: Chatswood, N.S.W. : New Holland, 2008.
ISBN: 9781921073342 (hbk.)
Notes: includes index.
                 Bibliography.
Target Audience: For primary age children.
Subjects: Inventions.
                 Discoveries in science.
Dewey Number: 608

Commissioning Editor: Yani Silvana
Designer: Tania Gomes
Reproduction: Linda Bottari
Printer: Tien Wah Press, Malaysia

Picture Credits
t = top, l = left, r = right, b = bottom,
c = centre, bg = background

Contents

Introduction

Our lives today are very different from those of our ancestors, centuries or even just decades ago. Although we do many of the same things—go to school, work, get married, raise a family, have fun with friends—we do them quite differently. Often this is because we use different **technology**.

People keep coming up with inventions and new ideas to do things better. Many of these, such as cars and aeroplanes, radio and TV, fast food, mobile phones and the internet, have become such a part of our lives that we cannot imagine living without them. But your great-great-grandparents didn't have them and in some parts of the world people still don't have them.

This book will tell you how many of these things were invented and where and when they were made. You will also find out about some of the people who made them and why. Maybe one day you will invent something that changes the way people live.

Everyday Inventions

Every day, in whatever we do, we make use of someone else's bright ideas. Our lives are full of inventions. Some make life easier and more comfortable; others are less harmful to the environment than what came before.

What's the Time?

Clocks have been around for hundreds of years, but they were the huge kind, like Big Ben in London, set into towers and powered by falling weights. Then, in about 1500, a German inventor called Peter Heinlein discovered that he could power a clock with a metal spring. Suddenly a timepiece could be small enough to put in your pocket, though the first watches looked a bit like turnips. Later came wristwatches, worn only by women until about 1900.

A Light in the Dark

Imagine if your street were lit by candles or gas lamps. It would be pretty dark and gloomy. That's what streets were like until the 1880s. After electricity was discovered, inventors like Thomas Edison and Joseph Swan passed an electric current through a fine thread of carbon, and it glowed brightly. They sealed the **filament** inside a glass bulb with no air in it, and made a light bulb.

*Light bulbs today have **tungsten** filaments, but are now being replaced by more energy-efficient fluorescent ones.*

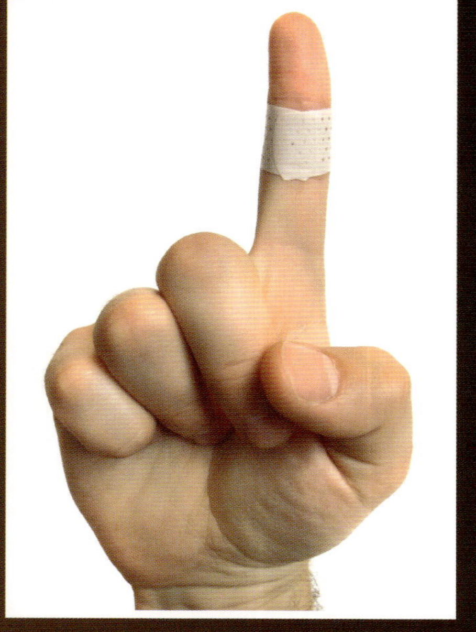

Instant First Aid

Before band-aids, if you cut yourself you would have to tape a piece of gauze over the wound—difficult to do on your own. In 1921 Earle Dickson wanted to help his wife, who was always cutting herself in the kitchen. He placed pieces of gauze at intervals along a length of tape, and covered it to keep it clean until needed. His wife could cut off a piece, pull off the cover and stick the dressing on. Earle's employers thought his invention a great idea and began to make band-aids by the million.

Sales of band-aids really took off when some samples were given to the Boy Scouts.

Lots of Tiny Hooks

In the 1940s Swiss engineer Georges de Mestral regularly returned from walking his dog to find they were both covered in tiny seeds. When he looked at them under the microscope he found they had tiny hooks that could catch onto things. So he made two pieces of cloth, one covered in hooks, the other in loops of thread. He had invented velcro. The pieces cling together, but you can easily pull them apart.

Velcro is useful on shoes and clothes—you can put on and take off quickly.

Pinning with Safety

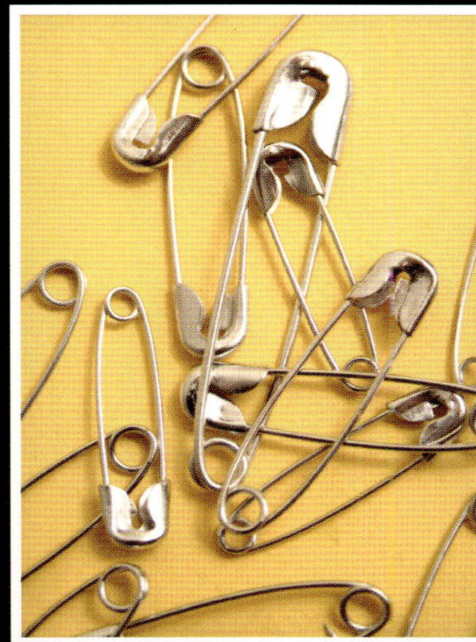

Pins were invented about 4000 years ago. But pins can come out and you can easily prick yourself. Then someone bent a pin in two so its ends could be hooked together. In 1849 American inventor William Hunt spent about three hours fiddling around bending wire. He wound the pin into a spiral spring, which put pressure on the latch to keep it closed. He sold his idea, the safety pin, to a friend for only $400 to settle a debt.

Strike a Light

People have used fire since prehistoric days. At first, they would rub two sticks together or strike a piece of flint to make sparks. A Frenchman called Chancel invented the first match in 1805. The head of the match was made with some chemicals, sugar and rubber. You had to dip it into a small bottle of sulfuric acid to light it—not a very safe thing to carry around!

In modern 'safety' matches, some of the chemicals are on the match head, and some on the box—when you 'strike' the match it lights up.

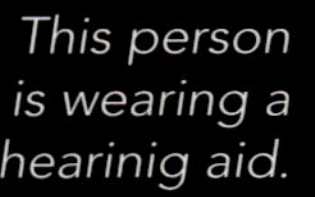

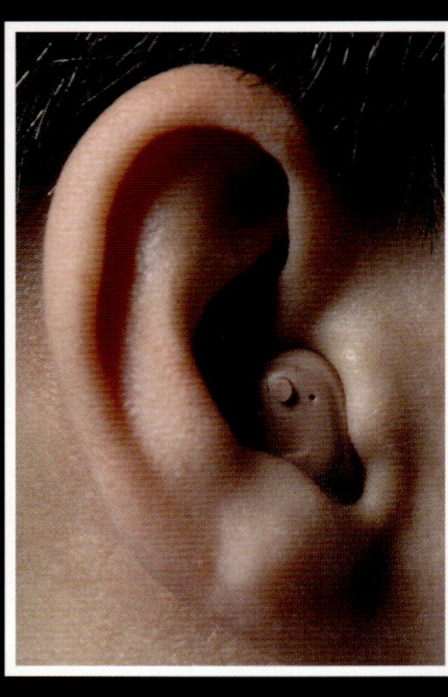

This person is wearing a hearinig aid.

The Deaf Can Hear

The chatter of friends; a great song; the crash of the ocean. Most of us take these sounds for granted, but some people never hear them. People can be born deaf or go deaf later, because of sickness or injury. Hearing aids just make sounds louder; they don't work for everyone. In 1978 an Australian scientist, Graeme Clark, invented the cochlear implant or 'bionic ear'. This machine turns sound into signals that are sent through wires to the brain. Suddenly many deaf people could hear again. Graeme Clark had to pay for his own research, so he spent lunchtimes standing on street corners shaking a tin to collect donations.

*Wilhelm Röntgen realised the importance of X-rays for the medical world, and won the first ever **Nobel Prize** for Physics for his work.*

What's Going on Inside?

For centuries, doctors had no way of knowing exactly what was happening inside a sick person's body. They could only treat the symptoms. The stethoscope, invented in France in 1816 by René Laennec, let doctors hear the sound of the heart clearly for the first time. Eighty years later, the first **X-rays** were used to look at diseased organs and broken bones. Today we have machines that can scan every part of our bodies, inside and out, and in 3-D. Doctors are no longer in the dark.

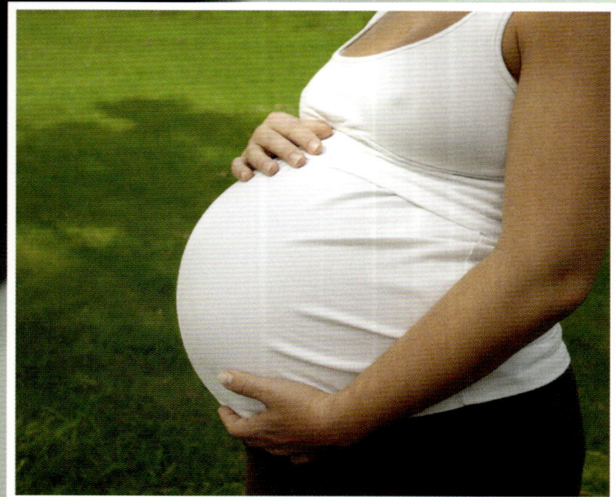

Making Babies

A baby is created inside its mother's body, when the father's sperm enters and fertilises the mother's egg. Sometimes this can't happen naturally. During the 1970s scientists worked out how to bring the egg and sperm together outside the mother's body. The fertilised egg is then put back into the mother to grow normally. This process is called in-vitro fertilisation (IVF) and although known as 'test-tube babies', the embryos are actually fertilised in a shallow dish, not a test tube at all!

Keeping Healthy

Being sick is no fun. Just a cold can make you feel rotten, and there are some serious diseases that can kill people. Many years ago doctors could only guess what was wrong; they could do little to make things better. Today we know much more about how our bodies work so we are much healthier.

The Enemy Detected

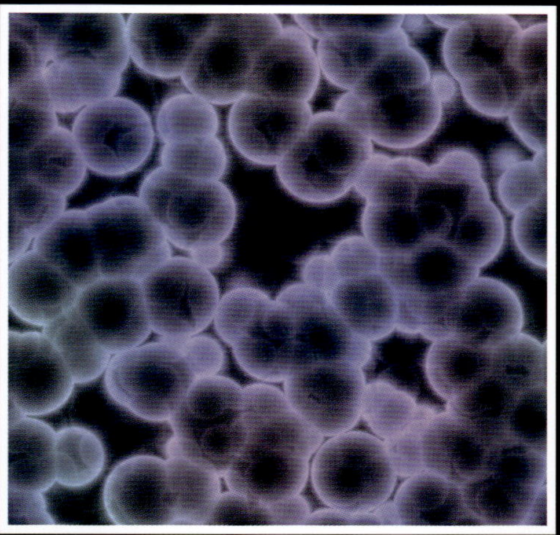

For thousands of years people blamed sickness on lots of things: bad air, too much blood, even demons. It wasn't until 1864 that Louis Pasteur discovered **bacteria**, tiny living things that can get into your body and make you sick. English doctor Joseph Lister then developed the first **antiseptic** to kill these germs during surgery. Years later, penicillin, a type of mould that stops bacteria growing, was discovered by Alexander Fleming. Today humans consume about 235 million doses of **antibiotics** like penicillin year.

Bacteria that cause disease are so tiny that millions could fit on the head of a pin.

Helping Your Body Fight

Your body has an **immune** system that protects you against many diseases. However, sometimes the body needs a helping hand. In the eighteenth century, Edward Jenner found that by giving people cowpox, a mild disease, they became immune to the deadly smallpox. A **vaccine** gives you a weak dose of a disease so your body is better able to fight it next time. You will have been vaccinated against lots of diseases so you are much less likely to catch them.

Doctors laughed at his ideas, but Jenner was so sure it would work that he vaccinated his own son against smallpox.

Sleeping Through Surgery

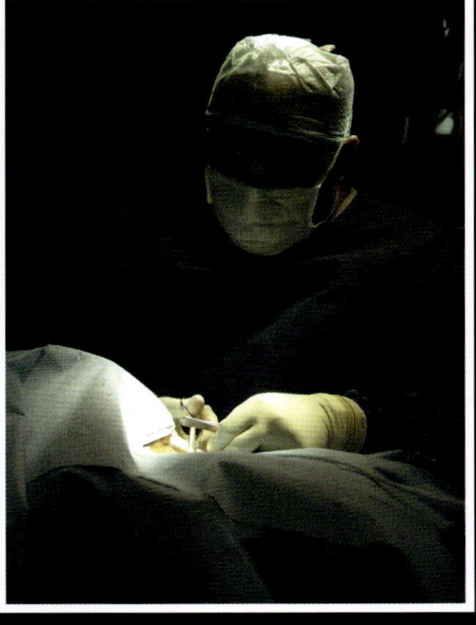

Imagine being awake while doctors operated on you! That's what it was like 200 years ago. Sometimes patients were knocked unconscious with a bang on the head—but the surgeon had to work fast and people often died from the shock. Relief came with the invention of anaesthetics, chemicals that make you numb or put you to sleep. William Morton was the first to use anaesthetic during surgery in 1846. With the patient comfortably unconscious, the doctor could take his time.

Modern surgeons do many wonderful things, but none of it would be possible without anaesthetics.

Getting Fed

Food is an essential part of our lives. You can only survive a few weeks without eating something. Finding food and keeping it fresh has always been important, and a string of inventions has helped. Once, people were simple hunters and gatherers, using spears and stones as tools. As **technology** developed, people became farmers growing food. The good ideas have continued to flow.

Remember Louis Pasteur

Have you ever found mould growing on a forgotten sandwich? Food goes bad when microscopic organisms, such as bacteria, begin to grow in it. Old methods of preserving food—drying, smoking, freezing, salting, pickling—kill, or at least slow down, those tiny creatures. In the 1800s, French scientist Louis Pasteur studied wine, beer and milk and showed that heating them quickly at a high temperature destroyed the bacteria in the liquid without altering the taste. We now call that process pasteurisation.

Louis Pasteur's obsession with bacteria meant that he wouldn't shake hands with anyone, even royalty, for fear of catching their germs.

Food in Jars and Cans

The greatest problem with fresh food is that it 'goes off'. In 1807, the French Emperor, Napoleon, worried about having enough food for his army. He offered a prize to anyone who could solve the problem. Nicholas Appert, who suggested sealing food in glass jars with cork lids, won the prize. A few years later, British merchant Peter Durand first preserved food in tin cans. But they were heavy, hard to open and made the food taste horrible! It took a lot of work before tinned food became popular.

The First Synthetic Food

Bread and butter have always gone together. In the nineteenth century, lots of people moved off their farms to cities to find work, and butter supplies started to run out. In 1870, the French king offered a prize for a cheaper substitute. Chemist Hippolyte Mège-Mouriez won with the invention of 'margarine'. It was made from animal fat at first, but is now made mostly from oil from plants like sunflowers or canola.

Margaric acid was discovered in 1813 by Michael Chevreul and named because the drops of fat reminded him of pearls, called margaron in Greek.

Potato chips now come in a huge variety of shapes and flavours.

The World's Favourite Snack

When next you enjoy a packet of potato chips (or 'crisps'), thank American chef George Crum, who invented them in 1853. Crum served chunky, french-style potatoes, or 'French fries', at his restaurant. When a customer complainec the potatoes were too thick, Crum sliced them very thinly, then deep-fried them so they were crunchy. The 'chips' were a hit, but it wasn't until automatic peeling and slicing machines were invented that they became a top-selling snack food.

Starting the Day Well

Breakfast is the most important meal of day, and most of us start with cereal. There are many breakfast cereals available today, but the first was Corn Flakes. They were invented in 1894 by the Kellogg brothers, who ran a health spa in America. Quite by mistake, some cooked wheat had been left to go stale. To save money, the brothers decided to use the wheat anyway. When the softened wheat was dried and rolled out, each grain became a thin tasty flake.

Under the Golden Arches

The name 'hamburger' most likely comes from the Hamburg Shipping Line, which brought immigrants to the USA in the 1800s. A popular meal onboard was a patty of minced meat fried with onions and served between two slices of bread. The McDonald brothers began making hamburgers in California in 1940. Their 'Speedee Service System' for making hamburgers, meant the food was fast and cheap, and their popularity quickly grew. Macca's now has over 30 000 restaurants in more than 100 countries across the globe.

Down on the Farm

Long ago most people 'lived on the land', growing their own food and raising animals on farms. Today we still need farms to supply us with fresh fruit, vegetables, grains and meat, but there aren't nearly as many farmers. Thanks to machinery and other helpful inventions, modern farms are much more productive than they used to be.

A combine harvester harvesting wheat.

Bringing In the Harvest

Harvest is the busiest time for farmers. Crops must be cut and the ripe grains gathered in a short space of time. Once, this was done by hand, using **scythes** and sickles, and a lot of the grain was lost. Machinery has made harvesting much easier. The combine harvester was invented in 1834 by Hiram Moore. This giant machine can cut a crop of wheat, put the grain into bags, and bundle up the hay, while the farmer drives along. Maybe in the future, farm machines will drive themselves using computers and **GPS**.

Breaking Up the Ground

Farmers once had to break up the ground ready for sowing with an iron or wooden plough, pulled by a horse, ox or mule. It was hard work and very slow. Today's ploughs are made of steel, which is much lighter, and pulled by a tractor. When Richard and Clarence Smith found it impossible to plough the rocky Australian soil in the usual way, they invented the stump jump plough in 1876. Farmers could now plant their crops without having to remove all the tree stumps first.

In some parts of the world traditional farming methods are still used, like this ox-drawn plough in a rice paddy field.

Food For the Soil

Plants, or animals that eat plants, make up an important part of our diet. As plants grow, they take **nutrients** such as nitrogen and **phosphorus** from the soil. The richer the soil, the better our food tastes. Frenchman Bernard Palissy studied **fertilisers** in 1550, finding that nutrients taken out of the soil needed to be replaced. Natural fertilisers such as manure, bones, dried blood, sewage and seaweed have always been used, but in the 1800s farmers began to use synthetic fertilisers made from chemicals.

Synthetic fertilisers make crops grow faster but they may damage the environment.

Making Milk

Cows make the milk we drink, but we have to collect it. We used to milk cows by hand, but machines are faster and cheaper. The earliest vacuum milking machine appeared in 1851, but it was Scotsman William Merchland, in 1898, who invented the machine that is commonly used today. Machines now also separate the fatty cream from the more watery skim milk, churn milk into cheese and cream into butter.

It took nearly 50 years to develop a successful milking machine—farmers were too scared to use their cows as 'guinea pigs' for new designs.

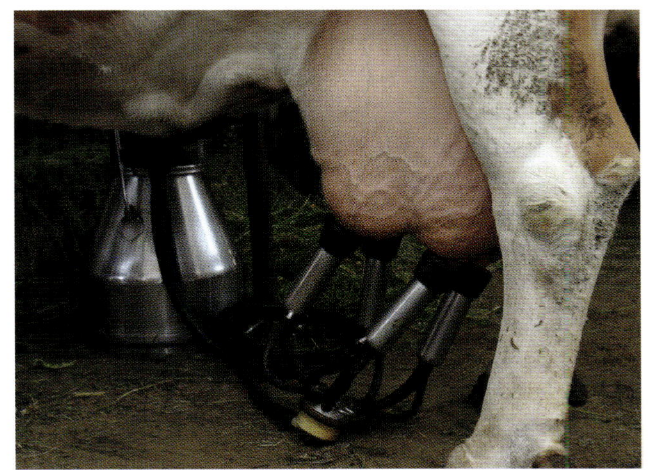

Over US$200 million is spent on barbed wire each year in the USA.

A farmer on a tractor sprays crops with pesticides.

The Devil's Rope

It was nineteenth-century settlers on the Great Plains of America who found they needed a new fencing material. Wood and stone, traditionally used for fences, had become scarce and expensive. In 1873, Joseph Glidden invented barbed wire, which was cheap, easy to use and stopped animals from escaping with its sharp spikes. Some people thought it was cruel, calling it 'Devil's Rope', but it did the trick and became very popular.

The Battle Against Pests

Growing crops is a constant battle against insects and other pests that want to eat them before we do. In the past farmers sprayed poisonous chemicals but these often did more harm than the pests. In 1996, **genetically modified** crops were introduced. These crops can be sprayed with herbicides, so that weeds die but the crop doesn't, or they produce their own insecticide. For example a cotton plant can kill off pests like the boll worm with a poison it makes itself.

What Ever Happened to 'Food Pills'?

Imagine if for every meal you just had to take a tablet. Years ago, scientists thought that by the year 2000 we would probably be getting all our food from pills made in laboratories or factories, instead of producing fresh food on farms. Although it is technically possible, most of us enjoy the look, smell and taste of real food too much to give it up.

Help Around the House

Most of us wish sometimes that we had servants to do all the housework and take care of the garden, like in the old days. But today everyone in the family pitches in to help with the cooking, cleaning, washing, mowing and raking. Fortunately we do have various inventions that make life a little easier.

Getting Rid of Dust

Before vacuum cleaners, brooms and dust pans swept up dust and dirt from the floor. British engineer, Hubert Booth, designed the first vacuum cleaner in 1901 – a huge machine on a horse-drawn truck. It parked outside, sucking up dust through long hoses fed through the windows of the house. Then, in 1907, janitor James Spangler attached an old fan motor and a box to a broom handle, adding a pillow case as a dust collector. This became the first portable electric vacuum cleaner.

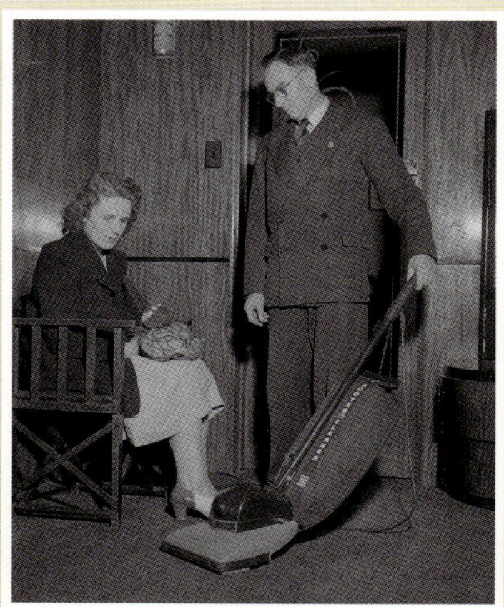

The first 'bag on a stick' vacuum cleaners were very basic, but before long almost every household had one.

From Grass to Lawn

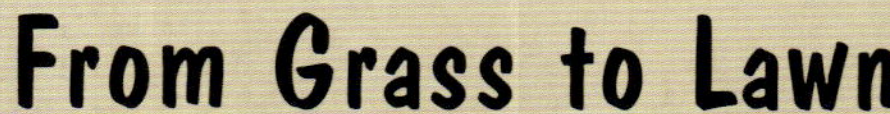

Lawns were once kept neat by animals that graze on them, or they were hand-cut with big shears. Edwin Budding designed the first mechanical lawn mower in England in 1830. Most early mowers were pulled by horses, which wore leather socks to protect the grass! Steam-powered mowers appeared in the 1890s, followed by petrol-powered machines. In 1899, American John Burr invented the rotary mower, which had blades on the edges of a disc rather than around a drum like the older mowers.

A father uses a hand-pushed mower around 1956, while his son helps with a toy mower.

Just Zap It

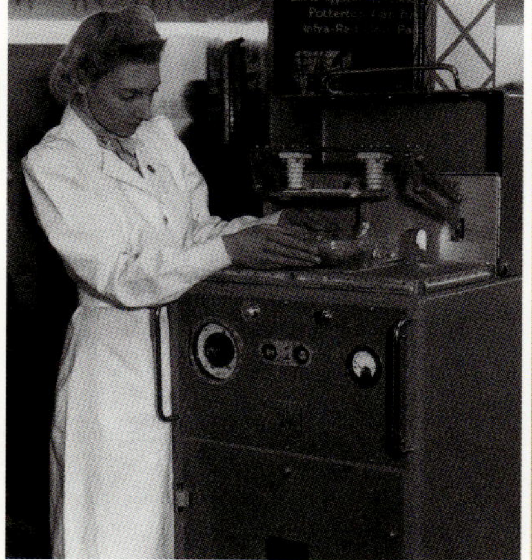

During World War II, scientists used **microwaves** in radars to detect enemy ships and planes. Several years later, Dr Percy Spencer, an engineer, was working with microwaves, when he found that a chocolate bar in his pocket had melted. He discovered that microwaves could cook food. The first microwave ovens were the size of a fridge, and cost thousands of dollars. A safe domestic oven for the kitchen bench was introduced in 1967, for only $500.

A woman using an early microwave at the Ideal Home Exhibition in London, 1947.

Detecting Smoke

What do you think is the handiest invention in your home? One gadget that the law now requires all homes to have is a smoke detector. The first smoke detectors relied on a wedge of butter melting in the heat of a fire to set off the alarm! Battery-operated detectors for the home were invented in 1969. They know that smoke is in the air when the level of electricity drops.

Keeping It Cold

Have you ever wondered why we keep food in the fridge? Ancient civilisations kept their food cold, packing it in ice and snow. We now know that the **bacteria** that cause food to 'go off' can't live in cold temperatures. It took a number of clever ideas from scientists in the late 1800s to finally invent a machine that could keep food cold indefinitely. The first home refrigerator appeared around 1911, but only in the last 50 years have they been cheap and safe enough for the average household to own.

Supermarkets need lots of refrigerators.

Getting the Clothes Dry

Hill's line wound up to catch the breeze. It was so successful that all his neighbours wanted one too.

Hanging clothes out in the sun and wind to help them dry faster and smell fresher is an obvious idea. However, old washing lines were long and straight, and wouldn't fit in small backyards. The answer was the rotary clothes hoist, first invented in Australia in the 1920s, but made popular by Lance Hill in the 1940s. The 'Hills Hoist' is shaped like a spider web, with the line around a centre pole, so it takes up much less space.

Washing and Wringing

When it was discovered that dirtiness brought disease, people realised they needed to clean up their act! James King invented the first machines to wash clothes in 1851. They were clumsy tubs with wringers turned by hand. When **electric motors** replaced hands in the 1900s, the person washing had to be careful not to get an electric shock as water splashed onto the motor. Automatic machines cost as much as a car at first, but became cheap enough for most homes to have one.

Unlike this rickety invention, where clothes had to be pushed through the wringer by hand, modern machines wash, rinse and spin dry, all with the touch of a button.

The Power of Steam

The steam engine was invented in 1698, but in 1769 James Watt worked out how to make steam even more powerful. Furnaces burning wood, coal, oil or gas released huge amounts of heat to boil water, just like boiling the kettle at home. The hot blasts of steam pushed on **pistons** inside **cylinders** and spun turbines, driving machines in factories, and powering ships and trains. Steam engines created new jobs and new ways to travel, making life very different for ordinary people. James Watt first used the term 'horsepower' to explain to customers how much work his steam engines could do.

An old, restored steam engine.

Petrol Takes Over

Early steam engines were heavy, messy and used lots of coal. They could power a train but were way too big for a car. In 1876, Nikolaus Otto invented the internal combustion engine, which ran on petrol, a cleaner fuel than coal. It was light enough to put into cars and motorbikes, but powerful enough to drive ships and huge machinery. Gottlieb Daimler was the first to install a petrol engine in a stagecoach, in 1885, creating an 'automobile'.

Daimler also built the first motorbike, attaching the new petrol engine to a wooden bicycle frame.

The Convenient Battery

Electricity is part of nature—you can see it as lightning, hear it as thunder and feel it 'zap' as you go down a slide. But for electricity to be useful, we had to be able to make it when we needed it. Through his invention of the battery, in 1800, Alessandro Volta did this, with a simple chemical reaction. Today batteries come in many shapes and sizes. Torches, mobile phones, computers and cars all need one. Rechargeable batteries can store energy and use it again and again.

The most common rechargeable battery is a lead-acid battery, found in every car.

Moving with Electricity

Have you ever heard the whirring of a motor inside your computer, or behind the fridge? In 1821, Michael Faraday discovered that a small engine could be turned by electricity using a magnet. Across the sea in America, Joseph Henry had also invented an **electric motor** using **electromagnets**. Those magnets were also in early electric **telegraph** lines, which sent messages before telephones existed. You will find electric motors driving all sorts of machines around your house, including vacuum cleaners, pool pumps and fans.

An old-fashioned electric fan, powered by an electric motor.

Endless Energy

In Australia the climate is great—warm, sunny days even in the middle of winter. And yet we don't use the sun as much as we should. It is a giant ball of renewable energy right there in the sky. The sun has been producing energy for billions of years, and we can convert that solar power into heat and electricity. In the 1830s, British astronomer John Herschel invented a device to absorb sunlight for heat to cook food during an expedition to Africa. Today we use solar panels to heat swimming pools and homes.

Solar panels on this roof generate electricity from sunlight without any waste or pollution.

Essential Energy

Energy is the force that makes things happen. You need energy from food to grow and move and think. Plants use energy from the sun. And machines need energy too. All our machines are using up too much of the Earth's **non-renewable** energy sources, such as coal and oil, so we need to learn how to use **renewable** sources of energy: moving water, wind and sunlight.

Water Energy

People have used hydro (meaning 'water') power for over 2000 years. You might think it sounds dangerous, generating electricity with water, but hydroelectric power is actually quite safe and environmentally friendly. Fast-flowing water is used to spin turbines connected to a generator—it never comes in contact with the electricity.

Catch the Wind

Wind is a renewable natural resource. Windmills have been used for centuries to collect wind energy for grinding grains or pumping water. Today wind **turbines** mainly generate electricity. Charles Brush built the world's first wind turbine for generating electricity in the USA in 1888. It was enormous—a 17-metre rotor, with 144 wooden blades. Despite its size, it only generated 12 kilowatts of energy, which Brush used to charge the batteries in his mansion.

A cluster of wind turbines together is called a 'wind farm'.

Materials Matter

Our ancient ancestors used natural materials to make what they needed—wood and stone, animal and plant fibres such as cotton, wool and flax, and clay baked into bricks or pottery. Today we have many more materials to choose from, many of them made by doing clever things to substances we find in nature.

Glass Grows Up

Glass is an ancient material, made for thousands of years by melting together sand and other minerals. Larger panes of glass used to be expensive and difficult to make, so windows were small—the richer the man the more windows his house had! In 1952, Alastair Pilkington devised a cheaper way of making large sheets of **plate glass**. By floating **molten** glass on a layer of molten tin, a perfect, continuous ribbon of glass is produced.

Some buildings look like they are made entirely of glass, though in fact they have steel frames to hold them up.

From Iron to Steel

Iron has been made for centuries by heating iron **ore** with coal in a furnace until the hot liquid iron runs out. The resulting crude iron had **impurities** in it and broke easily. Turning it into steel for, say, a sword was hard work and expensive. In 1855 Englishman Henry Bessemer invented a process for converting iron into steel much more cheaply. Our modern world is built on steel. It is in skyscrapers, railway tracks, in food cans, cutlery and machinery of all kinds.

A modern Bessemer converter in action. In Bessemer's first trial, white-hot molten iron erupted like a volcano from his converter, but it resulted in pure steel.

Abundant Aluminium

Steel is strong, plentiful and cheap, but it is also heavy and it rusts. Aluminium, too, is strong, but light and rustproof. Identified by Sir Humphry Davy in 1808, there is plenty of it in the earth, but it takes a lot of electricity to extract it from its ore, known as bauxite or alumina. So aluminium costs more than steel, but is certainly worth it where weight or weather matters, for example in drink cans, outdoor furniture, planes, trains and cars.

Aluminium cans are 100% recyclable.

The Secret of Cement

Cement was made by ancient Greeks and Romans, who mixed volcanic ash with limestone. This process was forgotten during the Middle Ages, and not rediscovered until 1759. When asked to rebuild a lighthouse, British engineer John Smeaton experimented with lime and clay, in search of the strongest cement. The fact that his lighthouse stood for 130 years proves he found the right mix! In 1824, Joseph Aspdin patented his 'Portland cement', which is now the world's most commonly used building material.

Cement mixers churn the cement all the way to the construction site, making sure it doesn't set before it's needed.

Piano-playing is still sometimes called 'tickling the ivories', but piano keys are now made of plastic.

Popular Polythene

Many plastics have names beginning with 'poly-', which means they are made from several small chemical parts joined together. Polythene, one of the most common plastics, was discovered accidentally in 1933. Made from the chemicals found in crude oil, it is used in everyday products such as plastic bags and cling wrap. Nylon, first produced in 1938, replaced expensive silk and is used in parachutes, women's stockings and toothbrush bristles.

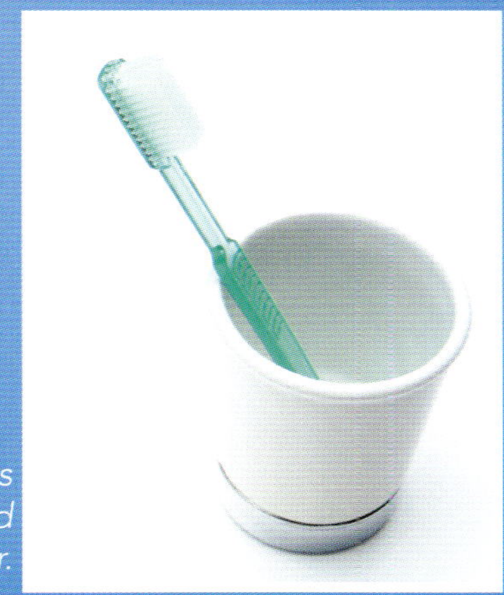

Before plastic, toothbrush handles were carved from cattle bones and the bristles were made of pig hair.

Fantastic Plastic

Synthetic materials, or **plastics**, are human-made substances that don't exist in nature. The first, 'vulcanite', was developed around 1843. Chemist Alexander Parkes improved on that, producing the first **thermoplastic**, which set hard but then softened again when heated. Then the American Hyatt brothers succeeded in creating celluloid, the first mass-produced plastic. Celluloid replaced ivory from elephant tusks in billiard balls and piano keys. Thin sheets of celluloid became the first 'film', making photography simpler and more popular.

On the Move

For thousands of years humans had only two ways to move across the land—either on foot or carried by an animal. Over water we could go faster, thanks to the wind in our sails. But to cover any sort of distance at a decent speed, we had to wait for the invention of engines running on steam and then petrol.

Pedal Power

The bicycle was the first real innovation for saving leg work! The earliest bicycle—or 'running machine'—was made entirely of wood and had no pedals. Riders sat and pushed the 'hobby horse' along with their feet on either side. In 1861 Ernest Michaux added pedals and iron-rimmed wheels, and the bicycle was born. But it was James Stanley, in the 1890s, who fine-tuned the design that became the model for your bike today.

The 'penny-farthing' was prone to accidents, as the slightest bump in the road could send the rider flying over the handlebars!

Steam Across the Water

From the earliest days of the steam engine, inventors dreamed of boats powered by steam replacing oars and sails. In 1802, after several failed attempts around the world, Scotsman Lord Dundas successfully launched the *Charlotte Dundee*, a paddle-wheeler with a steam engine. At the same time, American Robert Fulton built his own paddle-steamer and began a passenger service on the Hudson River, New York. Within a century, big steam ships could safely cross the Atlantic Ocean in a week or less.

Although paddle-steamers looked attractive, they were slow and uneconomical.

Sailing Under the Water

Submarines seem fairly high-tech and modern, but one fought in the American War of Independence in 1776. Designed by a college student, David Bushnell, and christened the 'Turtle', it was made of wood, carried only one man and had no engine. Today's submarines can be as long as two football fields. They are made of steel and are as heavy as 12 000 cars. They can carry a large crew and be fitted with powerful weapons. Some have engines driven by nuclear power and can stay submerged for weeks.

Nuclear power doesn't require air, so it is an excellent power source for submarines. Nuclear-powered submarines only have to refuel once every nine years.

The World On Wheels

Some say the motor car or 'automobile' is the most important invention ever, and it certainly is hard to imagine our world today without cars. Yet we haven't had them for long. In 1886, Gottleib Daimler fitted the newly invented four-stroke petrol engine to a stagecoach, and the automobile was born. His rival, Karl Benz, became the first to mass-produce cars. With the popularity of cars have come problems—pollution, traffic jams, road accidents—but most of us wouldn't be without one.

Cars may have been too successful—with over five billion now driving all over the world, it can be difficult to get anywhere fast!

We Take to the Air

For centuries humans tried to fly like birds. People flapped wings made of feathers or wood...often with disastrous results. We first took to the sky in 1783, in a hot-air balloon invented by the Montgolfier brothers. The Wright brothers then succeeded in building an engine-powered 'flying machine', and took the first flight at Kitty Hawk, USA, in 1903. Today, hundreds of people can travel in a jumbo jet to the other side of the world in a matter of hours.

Wilbur and Orville (at controls) Wright with their 1903 airplane at Kitty Hawk. Its first flight lasted twelve seconds.

Triumph of the Train

George Stephenson, a young British engineer, built the first steam locomotive engine for railways, in 1814, and travel changed forever. Trains were safe, reliable, punctual, comfortable, cheap and fast. A trip that took a week on a horse or by stagecoach could now be done in half a day. Almost 70 years later, electric and diesel trains appeared, followed by high-speed engines such as Japan's Bullet Train and the French TGV, which travel at speeds of up to 300 kilometres per hour or more.

Every part of the steam engine had to be made by hand, and hammered into shape. George Stephenson built 16 engines in all.

Journey into Space

As we walk around it, planet Earth seems a big place, but we now know it's really just a speck in the vastness of space. Over the last 50 years we have begun to explore the region around our home planet, using rockets to escape the Earth's gravity. With the help of complex machines, men have walked on the Moon and robot space probes have ventured further still.

War Came First

Since the Chinese invented gunpowder 2500 years ago, rockets have been used as weapons. The first big rockets were used during World War II. German-built V2s, one of Hitler's 'terror weapons', could carry a bomb hundreds of kilometres in a few minutes. During the Cold War that followed, military scientists concentrated on developing even bigger missiles, which could carry atomic bombs across the world. Thankfully they were never used. It was such missiles that began the Space Age.

German scientist Wernher von Braun invented the V-2 ballistic missile in the 1940s.

First Into Orbit

If something is fired into the sky fast enough and far enough, it won't fall back down. Instead, it will go 'into orbit', travelling around the Earth hundreds of kilometres up. The Soviet Union launched the first artificial **satellite**, *Sputnik* I, in 1957. About the size of a basketball, it took 98 minutes to orbit the Earth and was such a novelty that people ran outside to watch it pass overhead at night. Now thousands of satellites are in orbit and hardly anyone bothers to look.

*Communications satellites are used to bounce telephone calls, TV pictures and **internet** connections all around the Earth.*

Mars and Beyond

In order to explore space, special automated machines called probes were invented. Probes have been sent to nearly all of the planets, some taking years to reach them. The *Pathfinder* probe landed on Mars in 1997 to gather information. After landing, a small vehicle rolled out of the probe onto Mars' surface to collect data about the soil and rocks. Such probes also send amazing pictures back to Earth.

A rover explorer investigates the deserts of Mars.

Men on the Moon

The first satellites showed us what was out there; the next step was to go there. In 1961, Russian cosmonaut Yuri Gagarin became the first human in space, making a 108-minute orbital flight. Next stop was the Moon. Teams of **NASA** scientists worked for years to perfect the spaceship, the spacesuits, the lunar vehicle, communication devices and other equipment that would allow the crew of *Apollo* 11 to land on the Moon – and return safely—in July, 1969.

Neil Armstrong: the first man on the Moon.

A GPS receiver can accurately pinpoint your position to within one metre anywhere on Earth.

Where Am I?

Satellites orbiting the Earth do many useful things: they forecast the weather, send phone messages and transmit television programs around the world. They can also tell us where we are. The **Global Positioning System (GPS)** was invented by American Ivan Getting and the first GPS satellites were launched in 1974. A GPS handset picks up radio signals from a number of special satellites and works out its position on the surface of the Earth. Originally for military use, now GPS is the latest fashion accessory for your car!

The View From Up There

For centuries, astronomers have used telescopes to gaze at planets, stars and objects in space. But the view is far from perfect—images are blurred by the atmosphere here on the ground and there is too much background light. Outside Earth's atmosphere, where it is clear, the Hubble Space Telescope is in orbit. Since its launch in 1990, it has shown us the most amazing images ever taken of our Solar System, and of galaxies on the edge of the universe.

Galaxies on a collision course, photographed by the Hubble Space Telescope. The Hubble has photographed galaxies well over 12 billion light years away.

Who 'Invented' Flying Saucers?

In Texas in 1878, John Martin was out hunting when he saw a fast-moving object in the night sky. He said it looked like a large saucer. This was one of the earliest reports of an unidentified flying object. 'Flying saucer' sightings weren't common until the late 1940s, but they did exist. In fact, from November 1896 until May 1897 American newspapers were filled with stories about mysterious cigar-shaped objects with flashing lights. There were very few reports of UFOs before the 1800s.

Words on Paper

There is evidence of humans drawing pictures on cave walls as long as 30 000 years ago. From cave paintings came symbols carved on sticks or pressed onto clay tablets. Animal skins and then plant fibres turned into **parchment** were easier to use, but laborious and expensive to make. For much of history, the majority of people couldn't read or write, so the written word wasn't so important. It's very different now.

The Power of Printing

Imagine how long it would take to write all the Harry Potter books out by hand! Before the invention of printing, that's how books were reproduced. It could take years. In the mid-fifteenth century, Johannes Gutenberg invented a mechanical printing press, using blocks of metal letters, but it was still hand-operated and very slow. It was the invention of the steam-powered rotary printing press by William Bullock in 1863 that finally revolutionised the printing process. Printing speeds soared from 1200 pages an hour to 12 000 pages an hour.

Single wooden letters, and later letters cast in metal, first made printing as we know it possible more than 500 years ago.

Paper by the Kilometre

Paper is not a new invention. For centuries it was made one sheet at a time, using fibres from various plants, pressed and stuck together. Ancient Egyptians used papyrus. The Chinese invented wood-fibre paper around 105 AD. As more people learned to read, there was greater need for books and newspapers. In 1798, Nicholas Robert invented a machine to make a continuous roll of paper, greatly reducing production time and costs. From 1840, cheaper paper made from wood pulp took over, when Friedrich Keller invented a wood-grinding machine for the purpose.

It takes about 786 million trees to produce the world's annual paper supply.

Something to Write With

Paper isn't much use unless you also have something to write with. In the past, sticks and brushes were used. The quill pen, introduced in 700 AD, was made from a feather and dipped in ink. This was replaced with the **fountain pen** in the 1880s, but that still leaked and smudged. Hungarian brothers, Georg and Laszlo Biro, patented a new type of pen in 1930. Using tiny ball-bearings in the nib, 'ballpoint' pens, or 'biros', were less likely to clog up or leak.

Ink, invented by the Chinese, was commonly used from about 1200 BC.

Writing by Machine

The arrival of the typewriter changed the lives of office workers forever and opened up a place for women in the workforce. The first patent for such a machine was granted to Henry Mill in 1714. Later models can be traced back to American inventors Christopher Scholes and Carlos Glidden, working in 1868. Starting out large and clunky, typewriters became small and portable, then fast and electric. Today the computer keyboard is the only typewriter many of us know.

The original 'QWERTY' keyboard layout (have a look at the letters on your keyboard) is still the most universally popular.

Copy That

Chester Carlson always dreamed he'd invent something amazing. Inspiration struck him while he was working in a boring job. He often had to rewrite documents by hand, as the quality of the messy carbon copies of the time were not good enough. He started to work on an easier way of doing his job, experimenting in his kitchen until his wife objected to the smell of the chemicals! But his persistence paid off and in 1938 he patented the first photocopier.

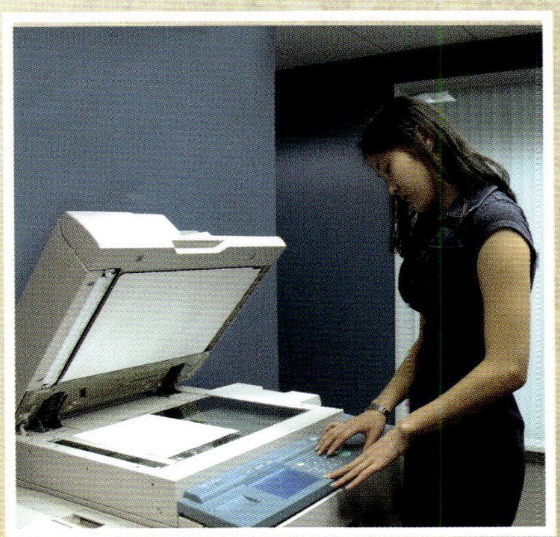

A small photographic company invested in Carlson's invention and went on to become the multi-million dollar Xerox Corporation.

Printing at Jet Speed

With the growing popularity of home computers came the need for a small, affordable printer. Older style printers were big, noisy and could only print in black and white. The inkjet printer was the answer: compact, fast, quiet, and able to print out full-colour photographs. Funnily enough, it was not originally intended for PCs at all, as in the 1970s, when it was developed, there were no such things. Released by Hewlett-Packard in 1988, inkjet printers are now the most popular printers on the market. Combined with a mobile phone and laptop computer, an inkjet printer becomes the 'go anywhere' office.

Keeping in Touch

Over the centuries people have invented many ways to get a message to someone too far away to shout to. These included smoke signals, talking drums, message sticks, carrier pigeons and waving flags. None of those methods let you say very much, and the message often was lost. From a man on a horse, to one on a motorbike, to the touch of a button on your computer—communication has come a long way.

It's in the Mail

Sending letters is not new. The Roman Empire developed a postal system using relay riders to cover great distances. In seventeenth-century Europe, the mail service was just for the king to use. Later, private letters could be sent via 'Royal Mail', but the recipient paid a fee. In 1840, the first stick-on stamps went on sale in England, with the sender paying the cost. Private letterboxes appeared in 1858, along with free delivery by 'the postman'.

Even with the arrival of email, billions of letters are sent by 'snail mail' each year.

A Message Down the Wire

Once it was shown that bursts of electricity could be sent down a wire, it was a simple matter to arrange the pulses in a code that represented letters. Then you could send a message long-distance in a few seconds, rather than a few days. American painter Samuel Morse devised the famous Morse Code of 'dots' and 'dashes' in 1838. Five years later, he built his first **telegraph** line. Long-distance communication depended upon the telegraph until 1877, when the telephone arrived.

Using equipment like this, a trained Morse code operator could transmit 40 to 50 words per minute.

Mr Watson, Come Here!

In 1876, American inventor Alexander Graham Bell spilt some acid on his trousers, and called for help. His assistant, Thomas Watson, heard his cries, not through the air but coming from the machine they were working on. It was the first telephone call! The 'telephone' (meaning 'distant sound') could carry sounds over a wire from one place to another. At first, calls were made through to an operator, who manually connected to the person being called. Automatic switchboards were introduced later.

You had to crank the handle of this antique telephone to make a call.

Walking While Talking

For many years telephones were attached to the wall or plugged in at a desk. You couldn't carry one around. The first mobile phone, invented by Bell Telephone Company, was actually introduced into New York City police cars in 1947. Modern 'cellular' phones weren't available until the 1980s. Even then they were the size and weight of a brick and could only send voices. Now they are pocket-sized, send 'text' messages, take photos and video, play music and connect to the internet. Dr Martin Cooper, a general manager at Motorola, is considered the inventor of the first modern mobile handset in 1973.

In only 25 years, mobile phones have become so popular that just about everyone has one.

Computer to Computer

While people were chatting to one another long-distance by phone, computers were starting to communicate with each other too. The idea of the internet, developed in 1973 by Vinton Cerf, was to allow researchers in different states across America to share information on their computers. British computer whiz Timothy Berners-Lee built on this to create the World Wide Web in 1989. Now people do their chatting on computers too, via email!

A world of information is at your fingertips—just 'Google' what you want to know and it will appear!

Talking Across the World

The first regular international telephone service, from New York to London using radio waves, began operating in 1927. A three-minute call could cost most of a week's wages. Telephone **cables** were first laid under the ocean in 1955, and in 1962 the Telstar international **communication satellite** was rocketed into orbit. Now a huge network of underwater cables and satellites in space whiz billions of voices and messages around so fast and so cheaply we hardly notice the cost.

Telecommunications dishes that communicate with satellites.

What's the News?

People have always been curious about what's going on around them—whether it's the strange noises coming from the next-door neighbour's house, or a war raging on the other side of the world. In ancient times, news was spread by word-of-mouth, through songs, stories and letters. Over the centuries people have invented many ways to spread information accurately and quickly.

Mountains of Paper

Nowadays printers and photocopiers make it so easy that we think nothing of printing out a few pages here, or copying a few pages there. The result is that we are being buried in paper. Newspapers, packaging and endless junk mail in the letterbox add to the pile. So it is important that we recycle anything we do not need to keep. One tonne of recycled paper can save 13 trees.

The News in Print

Long before printed newspapers, news of important events was passed from person to person on handwritten sheets. The invention of the printing press, in 1456, made these quicker to produce, but the first regular newspaper, *The Oxford Gazette*, wasn't published until 1665. The price of the paper never covered the costs, so even the earliest newspapers had advertising. Newspapers are now going online, and with the **internet**, millions of people around the world can follow important news stories as they happen.

What's black and white and read all over?!

Hearing the News

The first radio, then called a '**wireless**', was just for the army and navy to send important messages, particularly during World War I. In 1920, David Sarnoff's idea to bring entertainment and music (and advertising of course) to every home became a reality. Radio stations broadcast news and sport, at first by reading aloud from newspapers. In time, radio stations hired their own reporters to send in 'live reports' from where exciting events were happening.

Before television, families would gather around the radio for news and entertainment.

News with Pictures

People heard about major events and famous people on their radios, but they wanted to see them too. The first 'moving picture' news film was made by the Lumière brothers in Paris, 1895. The following year they sent a 'cameraman' on location to film international events: a bullfight in Spain, and the crowning of the Czar in Russia. Movie theatres began screening weekly newsreels from about 1911 until 1967 (when television took over), bringing the world coronations, assassinations, presidential elections and wars beginning and ending.

In the old days when you went to the cinema you got to watch the 'Movietone News'. This team of Movietone News cameramen is getting ready to film a big outdoor news event in 1938.

News on the Small Screen

Getting pictures for TV news was difficult at first with the large and clumsy equipment. Regular news programs went to air in the early 1950s. The assassination of President John F. Kennedy in 1963 was the first 'big' news story to be covered. And in 1969, 94 per cent of television owners tuned in to watch Neil Armstrong walk on the moon. Today communications satellites let us see important events from anywhere in the world as they happen.

A TV news team on the job in the studio.

News on the Net

The **internet** has changed the way we do most things, including getting our news. There are more details given than radio and TV stations have time to broadcast or papers have room to print. You can also access stories from newspapers and TV stations around the world. Many mobile phones have internet connection, so you can watch the news or catch up on sports scores whenever you need to, wherever you are. You could even watch the game while sitting on the beach!

The internet can bring news of big events anywhere, anytime.

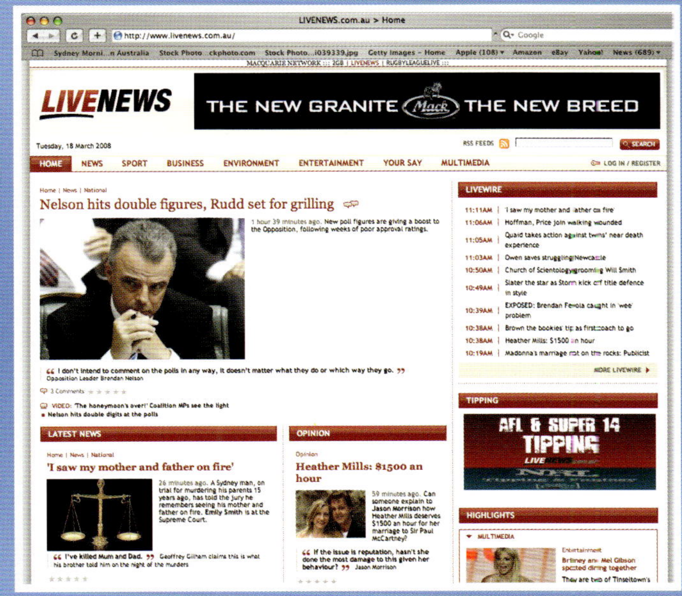

Smile for the Camera

We look at the world around us all the time, holding images of it in our minds. But those fade in time, and we cannot show them to others. Artists can create pictures in paint or stone, but they may not look like 'real life' and there is usually only one copy. Around 200 years ago people found a way for anyone to capture a permanent image they could share around. We call that photography.

The First Photographs

Photography began as chemistry, when scientists noticed certain chemicals went black when light fell on them. In 1839, artist Louis Daguerre spread those chemicals on silver or glass plates and exposed them to light. He was then able to 'fix' the images left by the light, including pictures of people and scenery. Making 'daguerreotypes' was slow and messy, and required a whole tray of dangerous chemicals, so it was for experts only. But the images were clear, and people started 'having their picture taken'.

A snap of photography pioneer Louis Daguerre, taken 150 years ago.

Everyone's Pictures

Around 1880 photography was transformed. Instead of cumbersome equipment and hazardous chemicals, George Eastman invented a small, convenient box camera called the Kodak—a brand we still know today. Images were captured on a thin sheet, or 'film', of the new **plastic** celluloid. The film was then sent back to the factory to be processed and the camera reloaded. It was not cheap but anyone could it, and increasingly they did.

Eastman said the word 'Kodak' had no meaning, but sounded nice, like the camera shutter opening and closing.

Pictures That Move

Once 'still' photography had become popular, people began to wonder if it were possible to photograph motion. They soon found that if you quickly flicked through a series of still pictures, each slightly different to the last, your eyes and brain were fooled into thinking the images moved. Using that trick, the Lumière brothers invented the cinematograph machine, and screened the first 'moving picture' in Paris in 1895.

A scientific trick became the multi-million dollar movie industry.

Sound and Colour

The movie experience today involves enormous screens in full colour with surround sound and special effects. However, 'silent' movies came first. They were in black and white, and had captions to help the audience follow the plot. The 'soundtrack' was played live by a pianist in the theatre. The Jazz Singer, released in 1927, was the first 'talkie' (film where you heard the characters talk) and **Technicolor** arrived in the 1930s. Yet despite all these marvellous features, the movie industry almost collapsed when television became popular.

Disney cartoon characters were among the first to appear in brilliant Technicolor.

Pictures with Pixels

For 100 years, all the snapshots we took used film, which took days to be processed. Hardly anyone bothers with film now. Digital cameras, entering the market in the 1990s, save the pictures in a tiny computer inside. You can look at them straight away, delete any bad shots and save the rest onto your computer or send them in an email. Digital cameras break the picture into tiny dots called **pixels**. The more pixels, the better quality the photo.

Digital cameras let you see your picture as soon as you take it.

DVDs can hold much more information than a video cassette, with room for the movie and a whole list of 'special features'.

Movies Move On

In 1971, Sony invented the video cassette, and you could borrow movies that you missed at the cinema from the video shop to watch at home. People were also able to record their favourite TV shows onto blank tapes. Now those cassettes have all but disappeared, in favour of DVDs (Digital Video Discs), which were first sold in Japan in 1996. The 'video' shop now only stocks DVDs and as it seems likely that movies will soon be available to download from the **internet**, there will be no need for the 'video' shop at all.

Cameras Do Lie

There is an old saying that 'the camera doesn't lie', and over the years photographs have been used as evidence of fairies, monsters and UFOs. That is not really true any more. With digital cameras and computers, it is very easy to alter a picture, adding details or taking them away, so it shows something quite different.

Money, Money, Money

Money makes the world go round: we earn it, spend it, try to save it. Money has no value in itself. It is only what it will buy that makes it valuable. It is the way we exchange one thing for another. Over the centuries we have invented lots of ways to make dealing with money easier, from the exchange of shells and animals, to credit cards and **internet** banking.

Ringing Up the Sale

On every shop counter and every supermarket checkout, there is a cash register to record the sale and calculate change. Today they are grey, functional computers, but early cash registers were ornate machines that rang up numbers from two rows of keys, then printed out a receipt. James Ritty, a saloon owner, was the inventor. Fearing his employees were helping themselves to the profits, he devised a better way to keep track of money and goods, building 'Ritty's Incorruptible Cashier' in 1879.

Ritty's design was based on a machine that counted how many times a ship's propeller went around.

Plastic Money

Nowadays it is possible to spend all day shopping and never touch a coin or note, just a small rectangle of printed plastic. Credit cards have been around for more than a century, although early 'store cards' could be used only in the stores that provided them. The first bank-issued credit card was invented by John Biggins in 1946. Today's cards are linked to central computers that keep track of the money and make sure the user is not overspending their limit.

Some people spend too much on their credit cards and find themselves in debt.

What Am I Buying?

Look on the packaging of just about anything you buy and you will find a 'bar code'—a small patch with a series of lines and numbers. This is like the product's signature. Invented by David Collins to identify railway cars, supermarkets also wanted to use the **technology**. After years of planning and spending billions of dollars, the bar code system was installed in 1974. At the checkout, a **laser** scans the bar code and the product is automatically added the product to the list of items you are buying and the store's product inventory updated.

Like a person's fingerprint, a bar code applies to only one product.

One Stop Shop

In olden days, customers would order items behind the counter and the shopkeeper would collect them all and measure them out. Service was slow and choices limited. In 1917, Piggly Wiggly in the USA became the first self-serve grocery store. In 1937 Michael J. Cullen opened the first real supermarket, in New York. Now, when we go grocery shopping, we wander supermarket aisles, piling our trolleys high from an incredible selection of food and household items, and have them scanned at the checkout.

Shopping in the supermarket is certainly quicker than shopping the old-fashioned way.

The Hole in the Wall

In the past, you found yourself in a spot of bother if you ran out of cash when the banks were closed (which was most of the time). Banks gradually increased their opening hours to try to meet customer demands, but it was the automatic teller machine (ATM) that really solved the problem. After ATMs were invented in the 1960s, people were finally able to have cash in hand at any time of the day or night.

ATMs were not an instant success, as people were afraid to let a machine handle their money.

Money and the Internet

The arrival of the **internet** has changed how we deal with money, as it has changed many things. You can do most of your banking online—check your bank accounts, pay your bills, apply for loans and move your money around. All this without having to leave the house and stand in a queue!

Computers

Everywhere

In human history, we have been through the Stone Age, the Iron Age and the Steam Age. Now there is little doubt we are in the Computer Age. Inventions that deal with words, sounds, numbers and images—creating them, storing them and displaying them—have changed the way we do just about everything.

A Computer to Fill a Room

Like many inventions, the first computer was built because there was a war on: World War II. Computers could crack enemy codes and help improve the accuracy of guns and develop atomic bombs. The first computer, or Electronic Numerical Integrator and Calculator (UNIVAC) as it was called, was huge. It weighed 30 tonnes and used enough electricity to light up a whole suburb! Information went into the machine, and came out again, on punch cards.

Built in the 1940s, this monster computer was a million times slower than the one on your desk.

Better Ways to Count

Counting began with fingers and toes and piles of stones. Then we began using simple devices like the abacus and more complex ones like the adding machine invented by Blaise Pascal in the 1600s. In 1974, we got pocket-sized calculators with batteries. They made maths easier for everyone, from school kids to scientists and accountants, but you still had to tell them what to do every step of the way.

Old and new ways of adding up; an abacus and a pocket calculator.

A Computer of Your Own

It took 30 years to get from the huge '**mainframe**' computers that only governments or big companies could own to the personal computer (PC) that appeared in the 1980s, cheap enough for one person to buy, small enough to fit on a desk. New **technology** like the **integrated circuit**, invented by Jack Kilby and Robert Noyce in 1959, had made that possible. Demand went up as the cost came down. Now computers are portable and getting smaller and more powerful all the time.

Sick Computers

One unwelcome invention of the computer age is the computer virus. A virus is a program specially designed to copy itself and 'infect' any computer it is sent to without the user knowing. Viruses can damage programs, delete files, or take up all of the computer's memory. The first PC virus was created in Pakistan in 1986.

Computers once got their instructions from 'floppy' disks; now they use programs on CDs.

Programs For Every Need

Computers are useful because they can be programmed. You can give them instructions through software on disks, and they will do what you want. Originally, computer companies like IBM supplied every customer with free software to go with their new computer. In the 1970s they realised there was a huge market for software sold separately. There are now programs for almost every purpose: word processing, drawing pictures, searching the **internet**, sending email, doing calculations, editing photographs and, of course, for playing games.

The mighty microprocessor: a complete computer as big as your fingernail.

Hidden Computers

In 1971, the world's first **microprocessor** was launched by computer company, Intel. Intel engineer Ted Hoff had worked out how to fit all the parts that made a computer 'think' onto one small chip. Now these tiny computers are everywhere: one controls the cooking cycles in your microwave oven; another changes the traffic lights; cruise control in cars is run by one, and space probes are carrying them far out into the solar system.

Making Music

Music has been a part life for thousands of years, in every culture. Inspired by the sounds of nature—birdsong, wind, water—humans found their musical voice. We need music to dance and to worship our gods. We sing songs to tell stories and express emotions. Musical instruments like pipes, horns and harps are among the oldest of all inventions. Electricity brought us rock'n'roll and now even computers can compose music.

Fingers and Keys

The pipe organ is the oldest keyboard instrument, invented over 2000 years ago. Harpsichords, popular in the 1500s, gave way to the piano around the turn of the eigtheenth century. The 'pianoforte' (meaning 'soft loud') was invented in Italy by Bartolomeo Cristofori in 1709. For the first time keyboard players could control the volume of the instrument, making much more expressive music. Modern electric keyboards might look similar, but have a computer inside, able to create an amazing array of sounds.

Invented by Edwin Votey in 1895, the pianola was able to play tunes by itself, by 'reading' holes punched in a long roll of paper.

Saving Sounds

Once played, music soon fades away. Not until the incredibly inventive Thomas Edison created the phonograph (meaning 'sound writer') in 1878, could we capture sounds, including music, to play back later. The first machines could record only three minutes of poor-quality sound. In 1887, 19-year-old Emile Berliner devised a system to record sound onto a flat disc, played on a gramophone. Recording quality and length improved and, most importantly, 'records' could be mass-produced using a master copy.

'Mary had a little lamb' were the first words recorded on a phonograph.

The Rise of the CD

For nearly 100 years people listened to music on vinyl records, which were easily scratched and jumped and clicked. But the old 'broken records' became a thing of the past when James T. Russell invented the compact disc (CD) in 1970. These use light from a **laser** to record and play back the music, instead of a needle as the old records did. As a result they sound better, play for longer and are not easy to damage.

The same laser technology is used for CD-ROMs and DVDs.

Music on the Move

Already the CD is in danger of being overtaken with still newer technology—the MP3. Developed in Germany, the MP3 first appeared in 1994. Each song is a compressed digital audio file, able to be downloaded from the **internet**. In 2001, Apple Inc unveiled the iPod, a tiny portable MP3 player. They are so small because the music is recorded not on a disc, but on a microchip. An MP3 player can hold hundreds of songs, as well as playing video clips and storing photos.

Now you can take your entire music collection with you wherever you go!

Fans for Free

While downloading music from the internet for free has caused a major copyright headache for recording artists and their record companies, it makes it easier for aspiring musicians to have their music heard. A band can have a huge number of fans without ever making a cd or performing live.

Wurlitzer jukeboxes, incredibly popular in the 50s, were first designed to look like a giant radio.

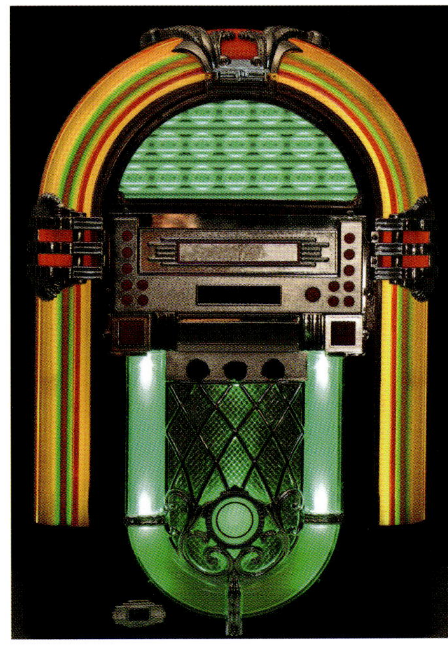

Music on Demand

In 1889, Thomas Edison invented the 'Nickelodeon'. Customers could put a coin in a slot to hear recorded music. This led to the jukebox, which really took off in the 1930s, when clubs needed music but couldn't afford live bands. Early radio only played 'respectable' music, so young artists, many of whom were black, relied on the jukebox to have their new style of music heard. Today the jukebox is still a cheap alternative to live music, holding up to 100 CDs.

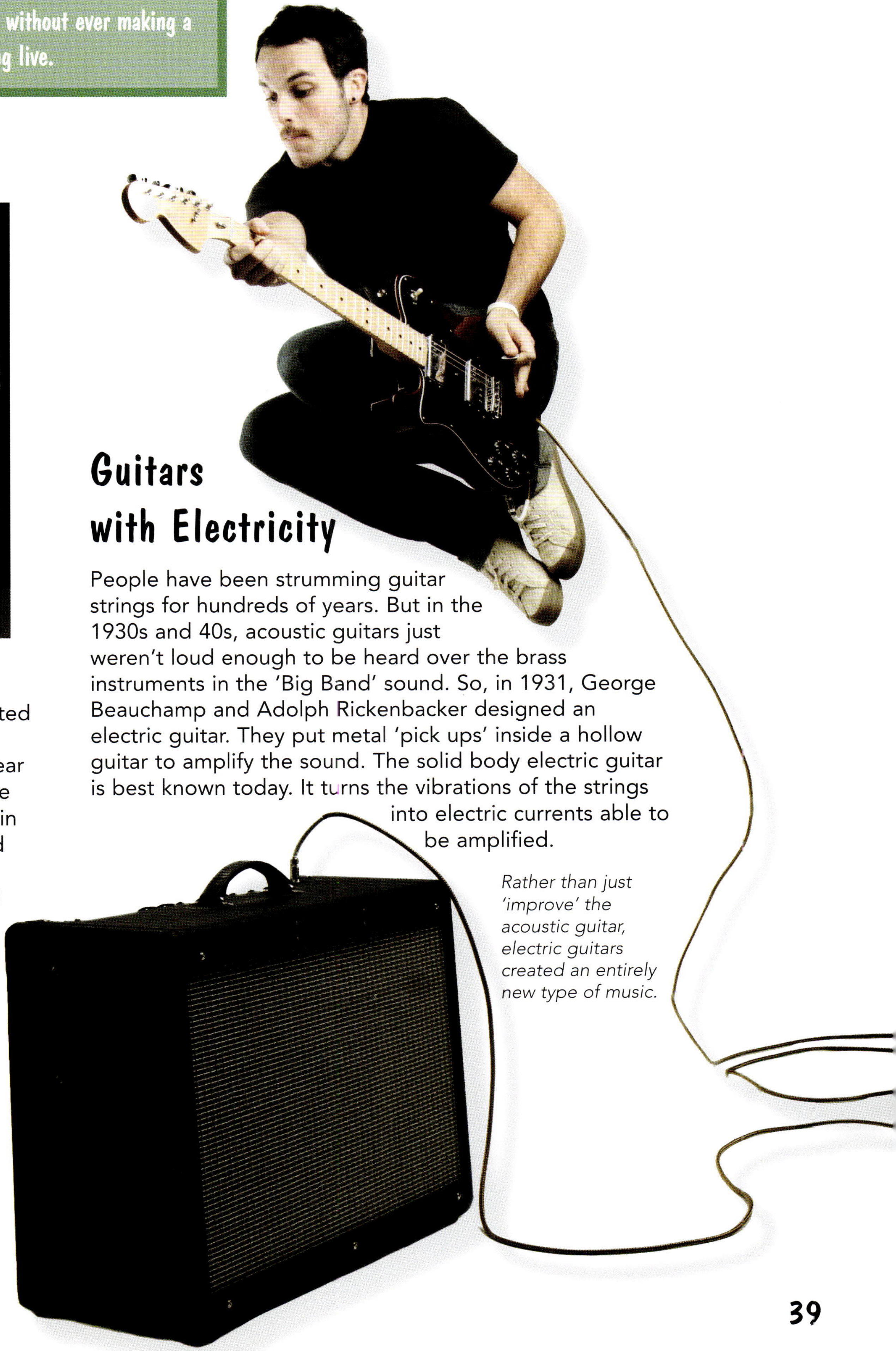

Guitars with Electricity

People have been strumming guitar strings for hundreds of years. But in the 1930s and 40s, acoustic guitars just weren't loud enough to be heard over the brass instruments in the 'Big Band' sound. So, in 1931, George Beauchamp and Adolph Rickenbacker designed an electric guitar. They put metal 'pick ups' inside a hollow guitar to amplify the sound. The solid body electric guitar is best known today. It turns the vibrations of the strings into electric currents able to be amplified.

Rather than just 'improve' the acoustic guitar, electric guitars created an entirely new type of music.

Fun Indoors

In times past, people spent a lot of evenings and rainy days inside with nothing much to do. Before electricity, and without radio, television or computers, people had to invent ways to amuse themselves. We still play some of these old games, such as chess and card games, and a lot of new ones too.

Ancient but Still Popular

Chess, or something like it, was invented in India around 600 AD, then spread to China and to Europe by the 1400s. Its rules have changed very little in 400 years. Russia takes chess very seriously, even setting up schools for promising young players. Playing cards, originated in the Middle East and became popular in fifteenth-century Europe. The cards often had beautiful, elaborate illustrations. Card games tend to be either a test of skill or a form of gambling, such as poker.

1500 years on, chess remains one of the most challenging games.

Just a Pencil and Paper

Some pastimes are perfect for one person to play alone. Crossword puzzles first appeared in 1913, and by the 1920s were being published in the daily newspapers. Still very popular, millions of people challenge themselves to complete one every day. A popular new number puzzle began as 'Latin Squares' in eighteenth-century Switzerland, re-emerged as 'Number Place' in America in the 1970s, then exploded in Japan in the 80s as 'Sudoku'! Kiwi Wayne Gould revived interest again in 2004 with his Sudoku-generating software.

*There are now **computer programs** for creating your own crosswords.*

Board Games Beat Boredom

The oldest and probably still most popular board game played by multiple players is Monopoly. Two hundred million Monopoly sets have been sold in 20 languages since it went on sale in 1935. It was invented by Charles Darrow, an unemployed salesman, who drew it up on his tablecloth to play with friends. Initially it was rejected by publishers, Parker Brothers, who thought it was too difficult and took too long to finish. In its first year, Monopoly was the most popular game sold in the USA.

People watch as a giant Monopoly board game begins in Hong Kong.

Play Well

Lego (meaning 'play well') is a Danish toy company that began in 1932, first making wooden toys, then moving into **plastic**. In 1949 Lego created their famous interlocking bricks that can be built into almost anything, but they were only available in Denmark. Lego as we know it today went on sale internationally in 1963. Since then most children in the western world would have owned, or at least played with, some Lego. Lego factories today produce 600 bricks every second.

A 3-metre model of a Star Wars rebel cruiser, made entirely of Lego.

Fun in the Arcade

You don't have to be at home to have fun indoors. Public arcades provide games you can pay to play. During the 1930s, people went to 'penny arcades' to find cheap entertainment. One of the oldest games is the pinball machine, where you fire a little ball around metal pins, hoping to win a prize. The first was built in 1931 by Raymond Maloney, who also invented poker machines. Pinball machines were banned in New York in 1942, seen as a form of gambling.

While pinball machines are still around today, most arcades are filled with video games.

Video Victory

Today, chess, cards, crosswords and Monopoly all take a backseat to video games. The very first interactive television game dates back to 1970 but it was during the 1980s that video arcade games, such as Pac-Man and Space Invaders, became hugely popular. Video games for the home took off in 1985 with the Nintendo Entertainment System, starring the famous Super Mario Brothers. Sony PlayStation was launched in 1995 and Microsoft joined the fun with its Xbox in 2001.

Video games are constantly being upgraded, and there is an enormous range of games for players of all ages.

Fun Outdoors

A familiar cry from parents through the ages has been 'Go outside and play'. When the weather is fine and we have some free time, there is nothing better than being outside, playing sport or just mucking around. Inventors have been at work here too, devising the rules of games, improving the equipment and coming up with clever ideas for having fun.

A Stick and a Ball

Lots of games involve hitting a ball with something: cricket, baseball, tennis, hockey, squash and golf. Most of these are only a century or so old. Lawn tennis was invented only in 1873, at a garden party. The rules of Cricket, one of the oldest games in its modern form, were written down before the First Fleet reached Sydney. The first cricket Test between Australia and England, played in 1877, was probably the first time two countries met on the sporting field.

Cricket is played mostly in countries that were once part of the British Empire.

Played in 200 countries, football is probably 'the world game'.

Many Forms of Football

People have been kicking footballs for thousands of years, originally using the bladder of a pig, filled with air and covered with leather. In 1855, Richard Lindon, a shoemaker, invented the modern rubber bladder. The English standardised the rules for soccer, the oldest of the 'football' variations, in 1863. Today soccer is the most popular game in the world. Other codes of football, such as Rugby Union, Rugby League, Australian Rules and American football came later as variations on soccer.

Skateboarding has influenced both fashion and music in recent years.

Skates and Skateboards

Skating on ice was a necessity for early humans, who carved ice skates out of bone. Modern steel skates were developed in 1865 by Jackson Haines. Skating on dry land took some creativity. 'Inline' skates were first patented in 1819. They then disappeared in favour of 'quad' skates for almost a century, but made a huge comeback as 'Rollerblades' in the 1990s. By then Californian surfers were fixing wheels under a wooden board so they had something to ride on when the seas were flat.

The Ball in the Basket

You don't have to be tall to play basketball, but it helps

Basketball is one of the world's fastest growing games. It began indoors, in 1891. James Naismith, a Canadian sports teacher, devised a game to keep a rowdy class active through the long winter. Points were scored by throwing a ball into fruit baskets sitting on 3-metre poles. Naismith soon substituted iron 'hoops' and mesh baskets, but it was ten years before open-ended nets were introduced. Until then someone had to climb up and get the ball after every shot!

Up In the Air

The trampoline is yet another attempt by humans to defy gravity. It was invented by George Nissen, a young gymnast, and his coach, Larry Griswold, in 1934. They built the prototype from an old canvas bed and rubber springs in Nissen's garage, and began commercial production a few years later. Trampolining became an Olympic sport at the Sydney 2000 Games. Recently, spring-free trampolines (invented by New Zealander Dr Keith Alexander) enclosed in retaining nets have increased trampoline safety and popularity.

Expert trampoliners can bounce to a height of 10 metres, staying in the air for 2 seconds.

Better, Lighter, Faster

Modern **technology** has had a big impact on sports. **Synthetic materials** are used in bats, balls, sticks and racquets to improve performance. Shoes and uniforms are constantly redesigned using newer, lighter fabrics. Races can be timed down to a hundredth of a second with state-of-the-art equipment to find the ultimate winner.

The Flying Pie Plate

Everyone loves a game of Frisbee on the beach.

Many people claim to have invented the Frisbee. Throwing and catching the circular disc has become a popular sport, even a competitive one (known as 'Ultimate Frisbee'). American college students discovered that the empty metal plates from pies made by the Frisbie Baking Company, could be thrown and caught, providing hours of lunchtime entertainment. The modern **plastic** version, engineered to fly further and more accurately than a tin pie plate, was invented by Walter Morrison in 1948.

Activities

1. Using the information in this book and other sources, draw up a table to compare the way people lived at the time of Queen Elizabeth I (400 years ago), Captain Cook (240 years ago), the time Australia became a nation (100 years ago) and now. Some questions you could ask are:

   • How would people travel to work?
   • How would they travel a long way (say, from Sydney to Melbourne)?
   • How would they cook their dinner?
   • How would they read a book at night?
   • How would they keep their food fresh?
   • What would their clothes be made from?
   • How would they wash their clothes?
   • How would they send a message to a relative a long way away?
   • How would they learn what was happening in other places?
   • How would they entertain themselves at home at night?

   What are some other questions you could ask?

2. Imagine that your great-great-grandparents came back to visit you, but they were only as old as you are now. (You will need first of all to work out how long ago that was.) Make a list of the all the things you would need to explain to them about, things that they would not even have dreamed about when they were your age.

   Get together with some friends and act out how you would explain those things, and the sort of questions your great-great-grandparents would ask you. Remember that they would have great trouble believing many of the things we have now are even possible! You could pretend to be your great-great-grandparents and explain how they did things.

3. Think of all the ways in which '**information technology**' (which includes telephones, television, photocopiers, cameras, as well as computers) has improved the way we do things, or has let us do entirely new things. How would people have done the same things before we had those inventions?

4. Imagine some of the things you would expect to see happening in the next 20 or 30 years, say, by the time you have children your age. What are some new inventions you would like to see? How would they make life better? Would everyone benefit from such inventions?

Glossary (what words mean)

Antibiotics	Chemicals produced by various sorts of mould that prevent **bacteria** multiplying and is made into medicine.
Antiseptics	Chemicals that kill bacteria and slow the spread of infection.
Bacteria	Tiny living things, invisible to the naked eye, which can cause disease and cause food to go bad.
Cable	A bundle of wires or optic fibres, either buried in the ground or laid on the ocean floor, that carry messages.
Cement	A vital building material made by heating limestone and clay ground together.
Combine harvester	A large machine that cuts and processes grain all at once.
Communication satellite	A machine in orbit around the Earth that relays TV, radio and phone signals across the world.
Computer program	The complicated set of instructions that tells a computer what to do.
Cylinders	The parts of a steam, petrol or diesel engine where the power is generated
Electric motor	A machine that uses electricity and magnetism to create movement.
Electromagnets	Devices that make a magnet using an electric current flowing through a coil of wire.
Fertiliser	Chemicals that can be added to the soil to provide the **nutrients** plants need.
Filament	A thread of fine wire that carries the current in a light bulb and glows when the light is switched on.
Fountain pen	A pen with a nib that has its own internal reservoir of ink.
Genetically modified	Usually refers to plants whose genes (inherited instructions inside each cell) have been changed by humans, altering their behaviour or appearance.
Global Positioning System (GPS)	This uses dozens of satellites to send radio signals to receivers on the ground; the receivers can then work out where they are.
Immune/Immunity	The power in living things to fight off bacteria and viruses that can cause illness. Immunity can be increased by **vaccination**.
Impurities	Substances that make another substance less pure, for example when dirt or **bacteria** gets into water.
Information technology (IT)	The use of computers in various forms to create, store and retrieve documents, pictures and sounds.
Integrated circuit	A way of making a piece of electronics out of a solid piece of material with no connecting wires.
Internet	A worldwide network connecting one computer to another, allowing information to be shared.
Laser	A machine that creates a thin, intense ray of light, very pure in colour, and with many uses in **information technology**, medicine and industry.
Mainframe	The first sort of computer, built over 50 years ago, big enough to fill a whole room and able to be used by several people at once.
Microprocessor	A complete computer printed on a single piece of silicon the size of your fingernail.
Microwaves	A form of radio waves that can heat up materials containing water, used in ovens that can cook very quickly.
Molten	Material in liquid form—for example molten steel—too hot to be a

	solid, too cold to be a gas.
NASA	The space agency of the United States of America (National Aeronautics and Space Administration)
Nobel Prize	The most important international prizes in science, awarded in October each year.
Non-renewable	Refers to resources such as coal or oil that take millions of years to be replaced.
Nutrients	Chemicals (natural or humanmade) that provide food for plants and animals.
Ore	A rock or mineral from which a metal like iron, copper or lead can be extracted, usually by heating.
Parchment	A material for writing on, made from animal skins and used before paper was invented.
Phosphorus	A chemical used in matches (the name means 'carrier of light').
Pistons	The moving parts inside the cylinders of steam, petrol or diesel engines, which then drive the attached machinery.
Pixel	A small piece of a digital picture that can be processed, stored and sent via the internet. When put back together, many pixels form the original image.
Plastic	A common name given to a wide range of **synthetic materials** that can be easily shaped into different objects.
Plate glass	Large thin sheets of glass made by floating the **molten** glass on a layer of molten tin.
Renewable	Refers to sources of energy or materials that are quickly replaced naturally as they are used (such as water in a hydroelectric dam or the energy of the wind or Sun).
Satellite	Any natural or manmade object that travels around (orbits) a planet. Our Moon is a satellite.
Scythe	A long blade at the end of a long handle, used to mow grass or cut down crops for harvesting.
Sickle	A small curved blade in a handle, used to harvest crops.
Synthetic material	Materials like polythene, nylon and melamine, which are not found in nature and are usually made from chemicals found in crude oil.
Technicolor	The business name for a process that makes movies in colour, invented in the early twentieth century
Technology	A general name for machines or devices that make it easier to do things, like travel, send messages, stay healthy or grow food.
Telegraph	A machine invented by Samuel Morse to send long-distance messages in code as bursts of electricity down a wire.
Thermoplastic	A synthetic material that gets softer as it is heated (thermosetting plastics get harder as they get hotter).
Tungsten	A hard metal that melts at a very high temperature. Used, for example, in the filaments of light bulbs.
Turbine	A machine that spins as steam, water or hot gases pass through it. Used to drive planes, ships and generators of electricity.
Vaccination	A way of increasing **immunity** to a certain disease by giving the patient a very mild dose of the disease.
Wireless	The first name for radio, as it let **telegraph** messages be sent without the need for wires. A term becoming popular again with new wireless technology.
X-rays	A form of radiation that can pass through solid objects like the human body and reveal what is inside.

Want to Know More?

Books

Ayesnu, Edward (ed) (1982). *The Timetable of Technology*. Marshall Editions, London.

Bender, Lionel (1991). *Inventions: Collins Eyewitness Guides*. Collins Publishers, Sydney.

de Bono, Edward (ed) (1974). *Eureka: an Illustrated History of Inventions from the Wheel to the Computer* Thames and Hudson, London.

Ellyard, David (2006). *Who Invented What When*. Reed New Holland, Sydney.

Ellyard, David (2007). *Great Inventions of our Time*. Reed New Holland, Sydney.

Rattray Taylor, Gordon (1983). *The Inventions that Changed the World*. Readers Digest, London.

Websites

http://en.wikipedia.org/wiki/List_of_inventors

http://en.wikipedia.org/wiki/List_of_inventions_named_after_people

http://en.wikipedia.org/wiki/History_of_technology)

http://en.wikipedia.org/wiki/Timeline_of_inventions

http://inventors.about.com

http://www.ideafinder.com/history/index.html

http://www.factmonster.com/ipka/A0004637.html

Index